Himalayan Cats

Animal Friends

By Jan Pfloog

Formerly titled

ANIMAL FRIENDS AND NEIGHBORS

MERRIGOLD PRESS • NEW YORK

© 1973 Merrigold Press, Racine, Wisconsin 53402.

Macaws and Parrot

A—Blue and Gold Macaw
B—Hyacinth Macaw
C—Scarlet Macaw
D—Blue-Fronted Amazon Parrot

Shell Parakeets

CONTENTS

Thousands and thousands and thousands of years ago, when man lived in caves instead of houses, he already had dogs to help him hunt. So dogs are our oldest and closest animal friends.

The dogs in the picture are Pointers, one of the kinds still used for hunting.

Here you see Burros, a very small kind of donkey. Though small, they are tough and strong and can carry heavy loads. Burros are used in the southwestern United States, Mexico, and South America. Donkeys of one kind or another are used in all the warmer countries of the world.

Whenever people live close to trees, they have Squirrels as neighbors. If there are stone walls nearby, people are likely to have Chipmunk neighbors also. Both become very tame if nuts or seeds are put out for them, and if they are not frightened.

Cattle are important friends of man. They provide us with milk to drink, meat to eat, and leather for shoes. Some kinds of cattle are raised especially to give milk; others are raised for meat.

These are Guernseys, one of the kinds that are raised for giving milk. Sometimes they are called the Golden Cattle.

On this page, you see one-humped camels. They are called Dromedaries and are used in desert countries to carry both people and heavy loads. Water is scarce in deserts, and camels can go without it for longer periods than horses.

Farmers like to have cats in their barns to keep mice and rats away from the grain fed to cattle and horses. After the cows are milked, the farmer always fills a pan for the kittens.

Our warmest winter clothes and blankets are made from the wool clipped from sheep. These animals also provide us with meat and a soft kind of leather. Mother sheep, which are called ewes, often have twin lambs. Father sheep are called rams.

Chickens were probably the first birds tamed by man. They provide us with eggs and meat. Some kinds are raised especially to lay eggs. Others are raised for their meat.

These Brown Leghorns are raised for their eggs.

On this page you see Bactrian Camels. They have two humps and live in central Asia where it gets very cold. Their hair grows long and thick in the winter, and so they do not mind the cold. They are used to carry heavy loads.

Ponies are small horses. These are Shetland Ponies which come from the Shetland Islands, where they are used as work horses. In other places, they are kept for children to ride.

The commonest tame ducks in the United States are these creamy white ones called Peking Ducks. They are raised for their meat, and their soft feathers are used for stuffing pillows.

Here you see tame Yaks. They are used in central Asia to carry
loads and to furnish milk, meat, and leather. Their long, soft hair
is used for weaving cloth. Because they are strong and sure-footed and
do not mind cold, they are useful in the mountains.

Just as farmers like cats around their barns to keep mice away, so people used to keep a cat in the house for the same purpose. Now mice cannot get into our houses so easily, but we still keep cats because they are such fine pets.

Goats are closely related to sheep. These are Toggenberg Goats and come from Switzerland. They are raised for their milk, which is very rich and good. Young goats are called kids and are very active and playful. They love to climb and jump and butt each other.

For hundreds of years Indian Elephants have been tamed
and taught to do heavy work. They are big and strong and
are so intelligent that, having once learned their jobs,
they need very little guidance. This elephant is piling teak logs.

36

Raccoons are animal neighbors that we seldom see because they usually come out only at night. They are very skillful with their hands and soon learn to take the lids off garbage cans in their search for scraps of food.

These white-faced cattle are Herefords and come from England. They are one of the kinds of cattle raised entirely for their meat. They give very little milk.

The Eskimos who live in the Far North, where it is very, very cold, use dogs to pull loads on sleds. These dogs have thick coats so they can sleep curled up in the snow. They are very strong and look like wolves.

Horses were not tamed until long after most other domestic animals, but they became one of the most important of man's animal friends.

This is a Thoroughbred mare and her colt. Thoroughbreds are the fastest runners of all horses.

Dutch Belted Rabbits have a wide white belt around their
middles. They are raised mainly as pets. Some kinds of
rabbits are raised for their meat, and their fur is used in
making felt.

In the Andes Mountains of South America, Llamas are used for carrying loads. They also provide meat, and their wool is woven into cloth for clothing.

These Peruvian Indians are taking their potatoes down to the market in the village.

Geese were tamed over three thousand years ago. They are raised for their meat. Their downy feathers, like those of ducks, are used for stuffing pillows. The birds shown on this page are Toulouse Geese and come from France.

The Reindeer provides the people of Lapland with meat, milk, leather, and warm clothing. It is also used to carry packs and to pull the Laplanders' boatlike sleds. The Reindeer in the distance are pawing away the snow to eat the lichens under it.

Turkeys are natives of North America, and wild turkeys still live in parts of the United States and Mexico. The tame birds you see here are Bronze Turkeys. Their plumage is the same as that of the wild kind, but wild turkeys have buff tips to their tail feathers instead of white.

Border Collies come from Scotland where they have been used for hundreds of years to herd sheep. This one is heading off a ewe that is running away from the herd. Sheepmen like Border Collies because they are smart and make fine sheep dogs.

Before trucks and tractors were invented, big, heavy horses like this Belgian mare were used to haul wagons and to pull plows and other farm machines. The farmer in the picture is plowing with a team of four of these horses.

59

Water Buffaloes are used as work animals in Southeast Asia. This farmer in Java is plowing his rice paddy with an iron-tipped wooden plow and a yoke of Water Buffaloes.

Hogs are raised mainly for their meat. They give us bacon and pork chops and roasts and sausage. Mother hogs are called sows, and the young are known as pigs. Male hogs are called boars. These red hogs are Duroc-Jerseys.

These are all Goldfish, even though some are not gold.
The wild Goldfish that live in China and Japan are not gold
either; they are greenish. But long ago the Chinese found some

that had gold spots, and from these they gradually developed fish that were entirely gold like the ones in the lower left-hand corner of the picture. From these all the others came.

Dachshunds come from Germany. Their name means Badger-Hound. They were first used to hunt Badgers and other animals that live in burrows. Dachshunds have short legs so that they, too, can go down into burrows. Now they are raised chiefly as pets.

Hamsters

ABOUT SOME OF THE ANIMALS

Title Page: Himalayan Cats are a fairly new breed that was developed by crossing Persian Cats and Siamese Cats. The size, shape, and long, silky fur of Himalayans are like those of the Persians, while their color is that of the Siamese.

Contents Page: The Macaws and the Blue-Fronted Amazon Parrot come from the jungles of South America.

Shell Parakeets, or Budgerigars, come from Australia. In its wild state, the Parakeet is green with a yellow face and throat. Because the wings and back are marked with black and yellow in wavy lines, like the pattern on shells, they are called Shell Parakeets. *Budgerigar* comes from an Aborigine name that means *Pretty Bird*.

Parakeets of blue, yellow, white, and other colors have been developed since the birds were domesticated.

One reason for the popularity of Parrots and Parrotlike birds as pets is that many can be taught to "talk." They are such good mimics of sounds that they can learn to repeat words, phrases, or whole sentences with surprising accuracy. Of course, since they do not know what they are saying, it cannot be said that they really *talk;* rather, they only say words.

8-9: We do not know exactly when and how man began to domesticate dogs. However, we do know that it happened during the Stone Age, which was given its name because people then used knives, axes, and spearheads made of stone. At that time, human families lived entirely by hunting, for they had no other way of getting food, and they needed animal skins for clothing.

We are certain, however, that when men built their first crude houses they had dogs living with them, and their children were probably playing with puppies. This was many thousands of years ago, long before any other animal had been tamed by man.

Dogs were first used to help man hunt because they could trail animals by scent alone. Also, because of their keen sense of smell, dogs could warn man of the approach of such animals as wolves and bears, which were dangerous to him. Dogs are still used for these purposes, and many kinds have been developed for special types of hunting. Pointers, for example, are used to hunt game birds. By scent, they find game that is hidden in grass or brush; the Pointers then stand stock-still, showing the hunter exactly where the birds are. Because they *point* out the game, the dogs are called Pointers.

Long after the dog was domesticated, man tamed sheep and goats, and his dog helped him to keep the herds together, to find lost lambs, and to guard them against wolves and other wild animals. Dogs like the Border Collie (pages 56-57) are raised especially to herd sheep.

Down through the ages, as man's way of living changed, his dogs changed too, and special kinds were developed to do certain types of work. Today there are many very different kinds of dogs of all sizes, shapes, and colors, doing many kinds of jobs. One of the most important working animals that we now have is the Seeing Eye Dog. It is trained to lead blind people so that they can travel about without human help.

From the very first, dogs have grown up with mankind in a special kind of loyal, affectionate partnership that man does not have with any other animal.

14-15: In this country and in Europe, cattle are now raised mainly for their milk and meat, but for thousands of years they were also used as draft animals to pull plows or loads in carts or wagons. They are still used for this kind of work in some parts of the world. Such work cattle are called oxen.

18-19: Cats were not domesticated until the first men who became farmers began to store grain for future use. Before long, mice and rats came to eat the grain. Those first farmers probably noticed that if wild cats lived nearby, there were fewer mice and rats about. Farmers then encouraged the wild cats, perhaps by putting out food for them, and in time they were able to tame their helpful visitors.

Farming began in the Middle East and in Egypt, and it is from the wild cats of those regions that our domestic cats are descended, rather than from the European wild cat, which cannot be tamed.

Cats have never been domesticated to the same extent as dogs. In a way, they are still wild animals and have changed very little in size, shape, and hab-

its. Cats are still much more like their wild relatives, the lions and tigers, than dogs are like *their* wild relatives, the jackals and wolves. To those who love cats this makes them doubly interesting as pets.

20-21: When man domesticated sheep and goats, he became a herdsman rather than a hunter. He no longer had to depend upon hunting, because his herds were a nearby source of meat and milk for food, and of skins and wool for clothing and tents.

36-37: Because elephants do not often have babies in captivity, young wild elephants are caught and trained. Even the older elephants can be taught to work.

44-45: The domestication of horses made great changes in human life. Travel became easier and faster, although not as easy or as fast as travel by modern trains, cars, and airplanes. Before the horse was used, people either rode in ox-carts, which were very, very slow, or they walked. Soldiers mounted on horses could move much faster and farther than when on foot, and this made armies more powerful. Even plowing and hauling were done more quickly, because horses, when pulling a load, walk much faster than oxen.

In time, three main types of horses were developed:

The fastest-running kind, which were used for riding. The best of these came originally from Arabia.

Bigger horses that were good runners. These were used for pulling the carriages in which people traveled.

The biggest horses. These were used to plow and to pull heavy loads (pages 58-59). Such large animals were first developed to carry fighting men, or knights, who wore heavy iron armor; ordinary horses could not carry so much weight.

Horses were so widely used as a source of power that we still use the term "horse-power" to measure the power of a motor or engine.

68: Golden Hamsters come from Syria. The cheek pouches of the one that looks as though he has mumps are stuffed with sunflower seeds. He will carry them off and hide them to eat later. The name Hamster comes from the German word *hamstern,* which means *to hoard* or *to save.* In Syria, wild hamsters are said to store, in their burrows for winter use, as much as thirty pounds or more of seeds or grain.